Inventory of Amphibians and Reptiles of Appomattox Court House National Historical Park

Technical Report NPS/NER/NRTR-2006/056

Joseph C. Mitchell, Ph. D.

Department of Biology
University of Richmond
Richmond, VA 23173

September 2006

U.S. Department of the Interior
National Park Service
Northeast Region
Philadelphia, Pennsylvania

The Northeast Region of the National Park Service (NPS) comprises national parks and related areas in 13 New England and Mid-Atlantic states. The diversity of parks and their resources are reflected in their designations as national parks, seashores, historic sites, recreation areas, military parks, memorials, and rivers and trails. Biological, physical, and social science research results, natural resource inventory and monitoring data, scientific literature reviews, bibliographies, and proceedings of technical workshops and conferences related to these park units are disseminated through the NPS/NER Technical Report (NRTR) and Natural Resources Report (NRR) series. The reports are a continuation of series with previous acronyms of NPS/PHSO, NPS/MAR, NPS/BSO-RNR, and NPS/NERBOST. Individual parks may also disseminate information through their own report series.

Natural Resources Reports are the designated medium for information on technologies and resource management methods; "how to" resource management papers; proceedings of resource management workshops or conferences; and natural resource program descriptions and resource action plans.

Technical Reports are the designated medium for initially disseminating data and results of biological, physical, and social science research that addresses natural resource management issues; natural resource inventories and monitoring activities; scientific literature reviews; bibliographies; and peer-reviewed proceedings of technical workshops, conferences, or symposia.

Mention of trade names or commercial products does not constitute endorsement or recommendation for use by the National Park Service.

This technical report was produced by the University of Richmond under Cooperative Agreement 4560-B-0003, Supplemental Agreement No. 3, with the Northeast Region. The statements, findings, conclusions, recommendations, and data in this report are solely those of the author(s), and do not necessarily reflect the views of the U.S. Department of the Interior, National Park Service.

Print copies of reports in these series, produced in limited quantity and only available as long as the supply lasts, or preferably, file copies on CD, may be obtained by sending a request to the address on the back cover. Print copies also may be requested from the NPS Technical Information Center (TIC), Denver Service Center, PO Box 25287, Denver, CO 80225-0287. A copy charge may be involved. To order from TIC, refer to document D-082.

This report may also be available as a downloadable portable document format file from the Internet at http://www.nps.gov/nero/science/.

Please cite this publication as:

Mitchell, J. C. 2006. Inventory of Amphibians and Reptiles of Appomattox Court House National Historical Park. National Park Service, Northeast Region. Philadelphia, PA. Technical Report NPS/NER/NRTR-2006/056

NPS D-082 September 2006

Table of Contents

Table of Contents (continued)

Figure

Tables

Appendixes

Executive Summary

This inventory was conducted at Appomattox Court House National Historical Park (APCO), Virginia, in 2003 and 2004, to (1) document 90% of the amphibians (frogs, salamanders) and reptiles (turtles, lizards, snakes) of APCO, 2) describe their associated habitats, and 3) provide park staff with conservation and management recommendations. Survey methods included visual encounter surveys, audio surveys, and road surveys; dipnets, minnow traps, and turtle traps.

Twelve species of frogs, 12 salamander species, five turtle species, five lizard species, and 17 snake species were expected to occur at APCO based on known distribution patterns in published literature. The proportion of species documented during this inventory was 75% for frogs, 83% for salamanders, 80% for turtles, 40% for lizards, and 47% for snakes. Total success for expected species was 79% for amphibians and 52% for reptiles. These success levels are below target levels; however, dry and variable precipitation patterns in 2003–2004, low encounter rates with very secretive species, and the history of intense land use at APCO likely contributed to the low species richness.

Six habitat types used by amphibians and reptiles at APCO were described from the field notes obtained during this inventory, and include grassland, mixed hardwoods and pine, mixed hardwoods, mixed pine, impoundment pond, floodplain pools, and streams. All habitats surveyed support multiple species, and most species use both aquatic and terrestrial habitat types. Habitats supporting relatively unique assemblages included mixed hardwood forests, impoundment pond, and floodplain pools. The combination of habitat types used by amphibians and reptiles at APCO should be viewed as a matrix of habitats embedded within the landscape, rather than as a series of separate habitat types. These habitats interact via movements of amphibians and reptiles and they should be protected and managed as a landscape complex.

Although this study documented less than 90% of the expected number of species for several groups, there are opportunities to register additional species. This can be accomplished in two ways by park staff; routine accumulation of digital photographs of road-kills or live amphibians and reptiles encountered with appropriate documentation appended to the digital image, and the use of natural history (animal) sighting cards filled out by knowledgeable visitors. Verification of new species records should be confirmed by a herpetologist.

The mole salamander (*Ambystoma talpoideum*) discovered during thus study is listed by the Virginia Department of Game and Inland Fisheries as a species of special concern. The discovery of this species in APCO is significant and represents a new county record. I discovered two populations, one in the riparian zone along the Appomattox River north of U.S. Rt. 24 and another in the Tibbs Ice pond. Management of these two populations of mole salamanders requires protection of both the pools and terrestrial habitat.

Recommendations for APCO resource management include: (1) additional species inventory for frogs and snakes; further work to document snake species at APCO should include the use of coverboards as part of its sampling plan; (2) evaluation of areas of the park where there tend to be high concentrations of box turtles (*Terrapene carolina*), mixed hardwoods, and the

Appomattox River floodplain for adverse impacts prior to opening them to recreational activities; (3) not allowing the public to release any animals that have been in captivity, and park management should educate park visitors on this issue; (4) monitoring specific habitats on a regular basis at APCO for the occurrence and persistence of amphibians and reptiles including hardwood forests, the impoundment pool, and the floodplain pools; (5) development of educational materials on the ecology, flora, and fauna, and their interactions with human history at APCO; (6) monitoring and control measures of park raccoon (*Procyon lotor*), populations should be implemented to protect all amphibians and reptiles, especially turtles and their nests; (7) development of a comprehensive natural resource management plan to conserve amphibians and reptiles at APCO; (8) evaluation of the problem of the mortality of reptiles and amphibians, especially turtles and some snakes, on U.S. Rt. 24; and (9) a view of long-term management of amphibian and reptile habitats at APCO within the context of the landscape matrix in and around the park.

Acknowledgments

Will Brown, Chris d'Orgeix, Todd Georgel, Elvira Lanham, and Lenny Leta assisted greatly in the field. I thank Resource Manager Brian Eick for providing the collection permit, pertinent maps, some descriptive text of the park, editing, and a variety of other forms of support for this project. I thank Beth Johnson, Sara Stevens, and John Karish, and the National Park Service for providing the funding for this project. Jim Comiskey helped greatly with editing.

Introduction

Over the past decade, the National Park Service has been working to establish what is now called the Inventory and Monitoring Program (I&M Program). The principal and simplified functions of this program are to gather existing as well as new information about the natural resources in the parks and to make that information easily available at different levels to park resource managers, the scientific community, and the public. Although some of the national parks in the United States have conducted field research on their existing flora and fauna (e.g., Braswell 1988; Mitchell and Anderson 1994; Hobson 1997, 1998; Forester 2000; Tuberville et al. 2005), many parks have never completed baseline species inventories. Where information does exist, it is often incomplete and inaccurate and sometimes includes species well outside of their native range (Mitchell 2000b). For park managers to effectively maintain the biological diversity and ecological health of their parks they must have a basic knowledge of what natural resources exist in the parks as well as an understanding of those factors that may threaten them. One of the first goals of the I&M Program has been to establish baseline biological inventories for vascular plant and vertebrate species in order to provide reliable species lists—a fundamental tool for management.

Beyond developing a documented species list, being able to associate species and their habitats within the parks is critical to planning and development of an effective land management strategy. Resource managers need credible information on species and habitat requirements to develop effective policies, guidelines, and management recommendations. Inventories that include locality, species richness, and population information will provide a valuable spatial database for managers to use for a variety of habitat-specific or site-specific management needs.

This report includes the results of a baseline amphibian and reptile inventory conducted at Appomattox Court House National Historical Park (APCO) in 2002, 2003, and 2004. APCO (705.4 ha [1,743 acres]) is located in the central Virginia Piedmont, in Appomattox County, 4 km (3 mi) northeast of the town of Appomattox. The entire park has hydrological links to the Chesapeake Bay via the Appomattox River, a tributary of the James River. Topography in this area is comprised of gently rolling hills, deeply weathered bedrock, and a few rock outcrops. The landscape varies from a stream floodplain and shallow ravines at about 183 m (600 ft) above mean sea level and terraces up to 253 m (830 ft) above mean sea level. Mixed pine and hardwood forests cover most of the park. Loblolly (*Pinus taeda*) and Virginia (*Pinus virginiana*) pine are the dominant coniferous species, while various oaks (*Quercus* spp.), tulip poplar (*Liriodendron tulipifera*), sweet gum (*Liquidambar styraciflua*), and other hardwoods occur in terrestrial areas, and red maples (*Acer rubrum*) and black willow (*Salix nigra*) occupy wetter areas. At least one shallow, ephemeral pond (a former ice pond) is located on the site and the Appomattox River floodplain contains a number of shallow water bodies used by a number of species. The park is approximately 70% wooded and 30% open field.

Biological resources of APCO include a wide variety of animals and plants characteristic of the Virginia Piedmont. At least 72 species of trees and shrubs occur in the park, as well as 60 species of herbaceous plants and vines (National Park Service, Brian Eick, Natural Resource Manager, pers. comm.). The composition of the fauna is unknown. For more information, see the park's Web site at www.nps.gov/APCO/nature.

A search of the literature and museum specimen records for Appomattox Court House National Historical Park confirmed a lack of information on amphibian and reptile species occurrence in the park. No museum records were found in the Smithsonian Institution [NMNH]) or other museums. There is no published literature on the amphibians and reptiles of APCO. Based on known distributions (Mitchell 1994; Conant and Collins 1998; Mitchell and Reay 1999), 24 amphibian species and 27 reptile species could potentially occur at APCO (Appendix A).

The APCO herp inventory was conducted on May 9, 2002 on an initial visit, and from March 13 to September 7, 2003, and from May 23 to July 31, 2004 (Appendix B). Project objectives were to: (1) document 90% of the amphibians and reptiles at APCO; (2) describe their associated habitats; and (3) provide park staff with conservation and management recommendations.

The inventory of amphibians and reptiles at APCO was conducted at all accessible portions of the Park. Appomattox Court House National Historical Park consists of one main geographic unit.

Six habitat types were described by field crews as being used by amphibians and reptiles in APCO[1]. Common and scientific names of the flora follow Radford et al. (1968). The habitat and microhabitat (location where animal was first sighted, e.g., under log, along pool margin, moving in open) was noted for each capture and observation.

Grasslands (GRA) - Open fields dominated by grasses that are mowed on a regular to irregular basis or other land uses that have removed the forest canopy and created small to large patches of grass habitat. These areas include mixed grasses (Bermuda grass [*Cynodon dactylon*], velvet grass [*Holcus lanatus*], sweet vernal grass [*Anthoxanthum odoratum*], and broomsedge [*Andropogon virginicus*]) and herbs (dog fennel [*Anthemis* sp.], St. John's wort [*Hypericum* sp.], wood sorrel [*Oxalis* sp.], and dandelion [*Taraxacum officinale*]).

Mixed hardwoods and pine (MHP) - Common wooded habitat at APCO, consisting of loblolly pine, Virginia pine (*Pinus virginiana*), and hardwood trees that include sweet gum, various oaks, and tulip poplar. Understory trees include American holly (*Ilex opaca*), dogwood (*Cornus florida*), and some red maple, and ironwood (*Carpinus caroliniana*). Vines include trumpet vine (*Campsis radicans*) and greenbrier (*Smilax rotundifolia*), with an herbaceous layer of Pennsylvania smartweed (*Persicaria pensylvanica*) and grasses (*Panicum* sp.). Downed woody debris varies throughout this habitat type. Many areas have a thin layer of leaf litter and bare ground is exposed in some places. Several ephemeral pools (natural depressions in the landscape that hold water for varying times during the year, usually winter to summer) occur in this habitat type, varying in hydrology from short hydroperiods (weeks) to long hydroperiods (> 6 months), but usually drying out by the end of summer in most years.

Mixed hardwoods (MHW) - hardwood forests at APCO lack a clear dominant overstory species, and include oaks (*Quercus alba*, *Q. falcata*, *Q. velutina*), tulip poplar, red maple, beech (*Fagus grandifolia*), and blackgum (*Nyssa sylvatica*). The understory consists primarily of American holly, dogwood, blueberries (*Vaccinium* sp.), and huckleberries (*Gaylussacia* spp.), and saplings of overstory trees. The herbaceous layer is generally sparse, consisting of partridge berry (*Mitchella repens*), Pennsylvania smartweed, grasses, seedlings of hardwoods, and occasionally loblolly pine. Downed woody debris is a common feature on the forest floor on a thin to moderate layer of decomposing leaves.

Mixed pine (MPI) - Loblolly pine is the most common species at APCO, but some areas are largely composed of Virginia pine. In some areas, hardwood trees (red maples and sweet gums) are scattered among the pines, usually as understory trees. Herbs are sparse and include Pennsylvania smartweed and partridge berry; vines include poison ivy (*Toxicodendron radicans*) and greenbrier. Downed woody debris is less common than in the hardwood sites.

---

[1] It is recommended that sampling location coordinates be cross-referenced with future vegetation maps to standardize habitat type nomenclature.

Ephemeral Pools (EpPL) - Several ephemeral pools (natural depressions in the landscape that hold water for varying times during the year, usually winter to summer) occur in the floodplain of the Appomattox River north of U.S. Rt. 24. They vary in hydrology from short hydroperiods (weeks) to long hydroperiods (> 6 months), but usually dry out by the end of summer. Flood events help to keep these elongated pools scoured out; some lack leaf litter on the substrate, whereas others maintain a deep layer of litter. A primary pool that dries most summers was formerly a small impoundment used to provide ice in wintertime. Tibbs Ice Pond provides a highly productive aquatic habitat for many amphibians and invertebrates. It is one of the most valuable habitats in APCO.

Stream (STR) - The Appomattox River bisects the eastern portion of the park and crosses U.S. Rt. 24 at Appomattox Wayside. This is a relatively narrow, shallow, sandy river, with several deep pools and undercut banks. The substrate is largely bedrock and some areas have patches of small rocks bordering the stream. Tree and shrub vegetation overhang the river in many places. There are few debris dams on the river within APCO.

Methods

Expected Species List Development

A list of species expected to occur at APCO was developed based on Mitchell (1994), Conant and Collins (1998), and Mitchell and Reay (1999). The final expected species list is composed of 24 species of amphibians and 27 species of reptiles (Appendix A).

Sampling

After an initial site visit on May 9, 2002, field survey work was conducted during amphibian and reptile activity seasons (late-winter to September) in 2003 and 2004. The field schedule is outlined in detail in Appendix B.

Many sampling techniques were used to conduct the inventory at APCO. Amphibian sampling techniques are described in more detail by Heyer et al. (1994) and Mitchell (2000a); reptile sampling techniques are described in more detail by Jones (1986), Mitchell (1994), and Blomberg and Shine (1996). The protocols may vary when applied to monitoring (Heyer et al. 1994).

Audio Survey

Audio surveys, detections of a frog species by its species-specific vocalization, were conducted during the day and also at night by listening for frog vocalizations at known wetland sites. Audio surveys conducted as part of this inventory were not time-constrained.

Road Survey

Road surveys are the collection of live or dead amphibians or reptiles on roads, driven by day or night.

Dipnet Survey

A dipnet survey is amphibian species detection through sampling with dipnets in aquatic microhabitats. The dipnets used in this inventory were D-ring aquatic nets with a fine mesh bag (Wards Biological Supply Co., Rochester, NY). This technique captured adults and larvae.

Minnow Trap Survey

Un-baited standard GEE minnow traps (Memphis Net and Twine, Memphis, TN) were set in shallow water with the upper 5–10 cm (2–4 in) above the water surface to prevent drowning of air-breathing animals. Funnel openings were enlarged to 25–30 mm (1–1.2 in) to increase capture success of adult frogs and semi-aquatic snakes.

Turtle Trap Survey

Standard turtle hoop traps (Memphis Net and Twine, Memphis, TN) were set in wetlands one day and removed the next. Traps used were (1) single-funnel opening with nylon mesh on three

76 cm (30 in) diameter steel hoops (nylon turtle nets) and (2) single-funnel opening with nylon mesh on four 50 cm (20 in) diameter fiberglass hoops (mini-hoop nets for catfish). Each trap was set with two poles on either side (opposite sides of the funnel opening). Each pole had an "L" hook imbedded at each end to hook into the terminal hoops; this extended the trap to its maximum length, ensured that the funnel opening was outstretched, and allowed easy setting in water. Traps were baited with a can of sardines in soybean oil; several holes were punched in the top of the can to allow the oil to dissipate the smell, but prevented the turtles from eating the bait. Traps were set so that a portion was above the water surface to prevent the turtles from drowning.

<u>Visual Encounter Survey (VES)</u>

Unstructured searches of selected habitats and microhabitats conducted by an experienced field herpetologist when the probability of encounter is high (appropriate weather and season for the targeted species). Visual encounter surveys are sometimes referred to as haphazard or random searching. Random searches, however, are seldom random, as an experienced herpetologist will preferentially search microhabitats that may yield results. Visual encounter surveys were conducted by walking in an unstructured manner through a selected habitat type and observing active amphibians and reptiles, as well as turning logs and other surface objects to uncover animals. Binoculars are used for searching water surfaces, logs, margins of wetlands, and basking places for frogs, lizards, snakes, and turtles. Visual encounter surveys conducted as part of this inventory were not time-constrained.

Animal Measurements

All captured animals were handled in accordance with National guidelines developed by the professional herpetological societies. No animals were harmed in the process and each was released at the site of capture.

All amphibians and reptiles captured were identified to species. Common and scientific names for amphibians and reptiles follow Crother (2000). Most animals were measured and weighed and their gender was determined. All measurements were recorded in millimeters and weights were recorded in grams. Body and tail measurements of amphibians were taken using plastic rulers, metric tapes, and calipers. Weights were taken with Pesola® scales and Ohaus Scout electronic field balances (Forestry Suppliers, Inc.). Animals seen or heard in the field but not captured were included in the database simply as observations (= present).

<u>Frogs</u>

Snout-Vent Length (SVL) was measured from the tip of the snout to the cloacal opening while the body was maintained in a straight line (i.e., making sure the sacral hump was flat).

<u>Salamander</u>

SVL was taken from the tip of the snout to the posterior margin of the vent. Tail length was measured from the posterior vent margin to the tip of the tail when the tail was original and complete (not broken). For tails that were broken or had regenerated portions, the original tail portion was measured plus the length of the regenerated portion (resulting in numbers such as 19+21).

Lizards

Straight-line SVL was taken from the tip of the snout to the posterior margin of the vent (anal plate). Tail length was taken from the posterior margin of the anal plate to the tip of the tail when the tail was original and complete (not broken). When tails were broken or had regenerated portions, then the original tail was measured plus the length of the regenerated portion (resulting in numbers such as 32+26).

Snakes

SVL was taken from the tip of the snout to the posterior margin of the anal plate with a metric tape following the body curves. Tail length was taken from the posterior margin of the anal plate to the tip of the tail. Broken tails were simply noted, as these animals do not regenerate their tails like amphibians and many lizards. Snakes were weighed in cloth or plastic bags; subtracting the weight of the bag to obtain the snake's weight.

Turtles

Carapace length (CL) and plastron lengths (PL) were taken with calipers (dial and tree) as straight-line measurements from the anterior-most point to the posterior-most point on the shell. The bar on the calipers was always parallel to the turtle's vertebral column.

Locational Data

Location data for Appomattox Court House National Historical Park was collected using Magellan 310 and 315 hand-held GPS units. Location information was recorded where an individual animal was caught or observed. When a defined terrestrial habitat area was searched, such as a field, a coordinate was taken at the center[2]. For wetlands (e.g., pond, seasonal ponds), coordinates were taken where minnow traps were set, resulting in a single coordinate at one point along the margin. Search area boundaries changed once a new habitat type was encountered.

Photo Vouchers

Photographs were taken of at least the first individual of each species captured using a Nikon 6006 SLR with macro lens and Fuji chrome Provia 100F slide film; slides were scanned at 300 dpi with an HP ScanJet 5370C slide scanner. Digital pictures were taken using a Nikon Coolpix 775 digital camera, set at 1600x1200 pixels (Normal). A list of photo vouchers by number and species name is provided in Appendix C.

---

[2] Whether terrestrial or aquatic amphibians and reptiles may move considerable distances through the habitat during daily or seasonal activities. Thus, single coordinates for area locations were deemed appropriate as long as the habitat was uniform.

Inventory Results

Twelve species of frogs, 12 species of salamanders, five species of turtles, five species of lizards, and 17 species of snakes were expected to occur in APCO based on available habitat types and known species distribution patterns (Mitchell 1994; Conant and Collins 1998; Mitchell and Reay 1999) (Table 1, Appendix A). The current inventory documented 19 species of amphibians and 14 species of reptiles. These include nine frogs, representing 75% of the frog species expected to occur in the park; ten salamanders, 83% of the expected salamander species; four turtles representing 80% of the turtle species expected to occur in the park; two lizards, 40% of the species expected to occur; and eight snakes, 47% of the snake species expected to occur there. A map of the locations where all amphibians and reptiles were inventoried is shown in Figure 1. Total capture success was 79% for amphibians and 52% for reptiles.

A total of 419 individual amphibians were captured or observed during this inventory (Table 2), and included 116 frogs and 303 salamanders. Totals include all individual adults, frog tadpoles, and salamander larvae captured or observed. Pond-breeding frogs (*Hyla versicolor, Rana clamitans*) dominated the frog fauna numerically. The most abundant treefrog encountered was the eastern gray treefrog (*H. versicolor*). Two species of ambystomatid salamanders dominated this faunal group numerically, marbled salamander (*Ambystoma opacum*) and mole salamander (*A. talpoideum*). These and the spotted salamander (*A. maculatum*) are the primary pond-breeding salamanders at APCO. Stream-breeding species consisted of two-lined salamanders (*Eurycea cirrigera*) and three-lined salamanders (*E. guttolineata*). Three of the frogs also used the Appomattox River for breeding, bullfrog (*Rana catesbeiana*), green frog (*R. clamitans*), and pickerel frog (*R. palustris*). Seepage and small stream salamanders were dusky salamanders (*Desmognathus fuscus*) and the tour-toed salamander (*Hemidactylium scutatum*). Two species of terrestrial woodland salamanders (*Plethodon cinerea, P. cylindraceus*) were encountered in low numbers.

Of the 62 reptiles that were captured or observed at APCO during this survey (Table 2), 16 were turtles, 16 were lizards, and 30 were snakes. Eastern box turtles (*Terrapene carolina*) were the most numerous species found at APCO. Individuals of three freshwater species were found: snapping turtle (*Chelydra serpentina*), painted turtle (*Chrysemys picta*), and eastern mud turtle (*Kinosternon subrubrum*). All of these were associated with the Appomattox River and its floodplain. Two lizards were found, both apparently abundant on APCO: five-lined skink (*Eumeces fasciatus*) and eastern fence lizard (*Sceloporus undulatus*). The snake fauna was the most difficult to sample. In APCO, ring-necked snakes (*Diadophis punctatus*) and worm snakes (*Carphophis amoenus*) were the dominant species and most were found in hardwood forests in the park. Several species were found in and along the Appomattox River, including the northern watersnake (*Nerodia sipedon*) and queen snake (*Regina septemvittata*). Black ratsnakes (*Elaphe obsoleta*) commonly occurred along forest and grassland edge. The other "black snake" (black racer, [*Coluber constrictor*]) occurs primarily in overgrown grasslands, but only one was seen in the park, however.

Table 1. Checklist of the amphibians and reptiles of Appomattox Court House National Historical Park, Virginia. Expected column equals number of species that should occur in APCO given distribution patterns and available habitat; Confirmed equals number of individuals observed or captured during the 2003–2004 inventory. Species that were confirmed but not captured to voucher with a photograph are noted as "obs" representing Observed.

Scientific name	Common name	Expected	Confirmed
Frogs			
Acris crepitans	northern cricket frog	X	
Bufo americanus	American toad	X	X
Bufo fowleri	Fowler's toad	X	
Gastrophryne carolinensis	eastern narrow-mouthed toad	X	
Hyla chrysoscelis	Cope's gray treefrog		obs
Hyla versicolor	eastern gray treefrog	X	X
Pseudacris crucifer	northern spring peeper	X	X
Pseudacris feriarum	upland chorus frog	X	X
Scaphiopus holbrookii	eastern spadefoot	X	
Rana catesbeiana	American bullfrog	X	X
Rana clamitans	northern green frog	X	X
Rana palustris	pickerel frog	X	X
Rana sylvatica	wood frog	X	X
Salamanders			
Ambystoma maculatum	spotted salamander	X	X
Ambystoma opacum	marbled salamander	X	X
Ambystoma talpoideum	mole salamander	X	X
Desmognathus fuscus	dusky salamander	X	X
Eurycea cirrigera	southern two-lined salamander	X	X
Eurycea guttolineata	three-lined salamander	X	X
Hemidactylium scutatum	four-toed salamander	X	X
Notophthalmus viridescens	red-spotted newt	X	X
Plethodon cylindraceus	white-spotted slimy salamander	X	X
Plethodon cinereus	red-backed salamander	X	X
Pseudotriton montanus	eastern mud salamander	X	
Pseudotriton ruber	northern red salamander	X	
Turtles			
Chelydra serpentina	common snapping turtle	X	X
Chrysemys picta	eastern painted turtle	X	X
Kinosternon subrubrum	eastern mud turtle	X	X
Sternotherus odoratus	stinkpot	X	
Terrapene carolina	eastern box turtle	X	X
Lizards			
Cnemidophorus sexlineatus	six-lined racerunner	X	
Eumeces fasciatus	five-lined skink	X	X
Eumeces laticeps	broad-headed skink	X	
Sceloporus undulatus	eastern fence lizard	X	X
Scincella lateralis	ground skink	X	
Snakes			
Agkistrodon contortrix	northern copperhead	X	
Carphophis amoenus	eastern worm snake	X	X
Coluber constrictor	northern black racer	X	obs
Diadophis punctatus	northern ring-necked snake	X	X
Elaphe guttata	corn snake	X	
Elaphe obsoleta	black ratsnake	X	X

10

Table 1. Checklist of the amphibians and reptiles of Appomattox Court House National Historical Park, Virginia. Expected column equals number of species that should occur in APCO given distribution patterns and available habitat; Confirmed equals number of individuals observed or captured during the 2003–2004 inventory. Species that were confirmed but not captured to voucher with a photograph are noted as "obs" representing Observed (continued).

Scientific name	Common name	Expected	Confirmed
Snakes (continued)			
Heterodon platirhinos	eastern hog-nosed snake	X	
Lampropeltis calligaster	mole kingsnake	X	
Lampropeltis getula	eastern kingsnake	X	
Nerodia sipedon	northern watersnake	X	X
Opheodrys aestivus	rough greensnake	X	
Regina septemvittata	queen snake	X	X
Storeria dekayi	northern brownsnake	X	X
Storeria occipitomaculata	red-bellied snake	X	
Thamnophis sauritus	eastern ribbonsnake	X	
Thamnophis sirtalis	common gartersnake	X	X
Virginia valeriae	smooth earthsnake	X	

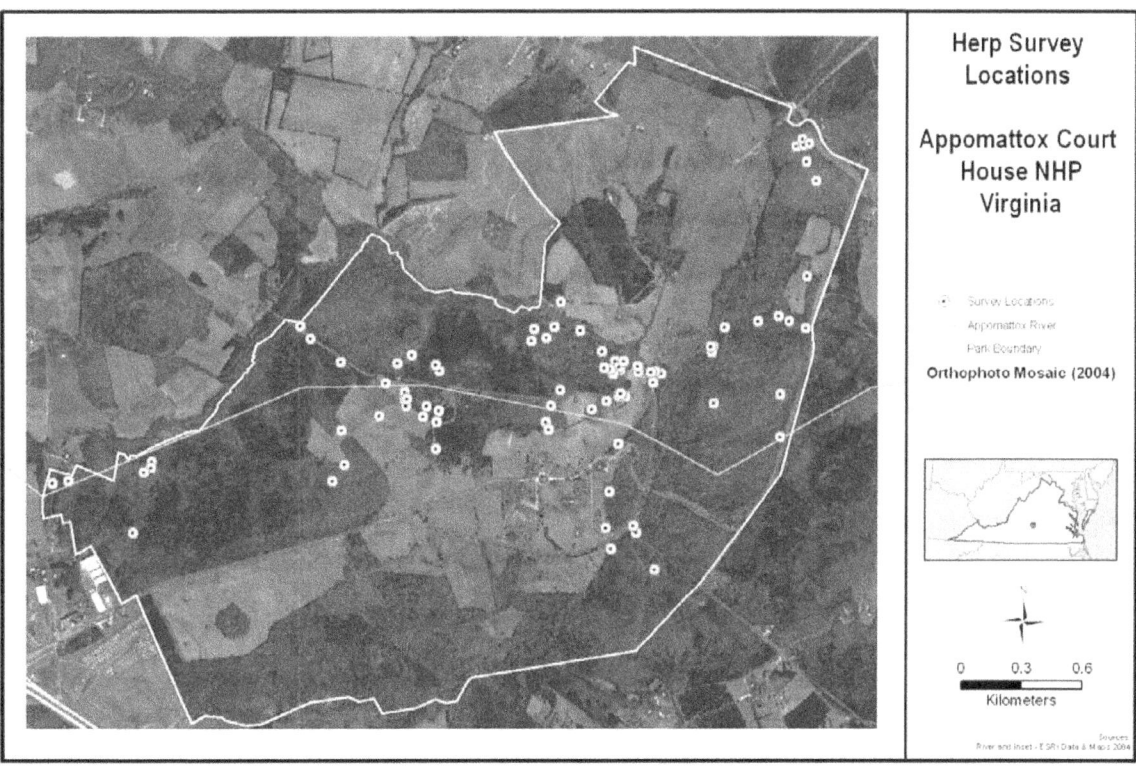

Figure 1. Map showing observation and capture locations for amphibians and reptiles in Appomattox Court House National Historical Park.

Table 2. Numbers of individuals of each herpetological species documented by sampling methods at Appomattox Court House National Historical Park during 2003 and 2004 inventories. The numbers in parentheses are individuals that were observed by park visitors and staff, including those provided in 2002 by Brian Eick, APCO Natural Resource Manager.

Scientific name	Audio	Road	Dipnet	Minnow Trap	Turtle Trap	VES
Frogs						
Bufo americanus	1	1				2
Hyla chrysoscelis	1					
Hyla versicolor	7		23	8		2
Pseudacris crucifer	3					7
Pseudacris feriarum	3					2
Rana catesbeiana	1					2
Rana clamitans			30			2
Rana palustris						5
Rana sylvatica			1			1
Salamanders						
Ambystoma maculatum			30			10
Ambystoma opacum			121			3
Ambystoma talpoideum			49	63		1
Desmognathus fuscus						4
Eurycea cirrigera						17
Eurycea guttolineata						2
Hemidactylium scutatum						2
Notophthalmus viridescens			3			1
Plethodon cinereus						1
Plethodon cylindraceus						1
Turtles						
Chelydra serpentina					1	(2)
Chrysemys picta						2 (1)
Kinosternon subrubrum						1
Terrapene carolina						12 (1)
Lizards						
Eumeces fasciatus						8 (1)
Sceloporus undulatus						8
Snakes						
Carphophis amoenus						10
Coluber constrictor						1 (1)
Diadophis punctatus						10
Elaphe obsoleta						3 (1)
Nerodia sipedon						2
Regina septemvittata						2
Storeria dekayi						1
Thamnophis sirtalis						1 (2)
Totals	16	1	257	71	1	126 (9)

No state or federally threatened species were found during this inventory. No venomous snakes were found during this survey, but the probability of the northern copperhead (*Agkistrodon contortrix*) occurring at APCO is likely moderate to high.

Sampling Success

The number of individuals of each species documented at APCO in relation to the sampling methods used is provided in Table 2. More species were detected using the visual encounter survey protocol than any other protocol (30 of the 33 species encountered in 2003 and 2004). Frog vocalizations resulted in one species not encountered using VES (Cope's gray treefrog, [*Hyla chrysoscelis*]). The dipnet and VES methods combined revealed three frog species not encountered by any other method (*Rana clamitans, R. palustris, R. sylvatica*). All salamanders were revealed by either dipnet sampling or by the VES method. All but one turtle species were found during VES surveys; the snapping turtle was found only in turtle traps. All lizards and snakes were encountered by the VES method.

Species/Habitat Associations

Capture and observation records for amphibians and reptiles distributed among six habitat types revealed that no species is a habitat specialist at APCO (Table 3). However, three habitat types in this park support a high diversity of amphibians and reptiles. These are the mixed hardwoods, the isolated ephemeral pond (Tibbs Ice Pond), and the pools in the floodplain bottomlands of the Appomattox River at APCO. The mixed-hardwood forests support a wide diversity of amphibians and reptiles, whereas amphibians dominate the other two habitat types. Several species of amphibians and reptiles are primarily associated with the Appomattox River and its riparian zone. Pine stands support very few amphibians and reptiles.

Amphibian species with five or more records confined to a single habitat type included eastern gray treefrogs in mixed hardwoods, ephemeral pond, and floodplain pools; spring peepers (*Pseudacris crucifer*) in the ephemeral pond; green frogs in the river floodplain; spotted salamanders, marbled salamanders, and mole salamanders in Tibbs Ice Pond and floodplain pools; and southern two-lined salamanders in the river floodplain. Reptile species with five or more occurrences in a single habitat type included the eastern box turtle, eastern worm snake, and northern ring-necked snakes in mixed hardwoods.

Table 3. Numbers of individual amphibian and reptiles captured or observed among six habitat types[1] at Appomattox Court House National Historical Park during 2003 and 2004.

Scientific name	GRA	MHP	MHW	MPI	EpPL	STR
Frogs						
Bufo americanus	2		1	1		
Hyla chrysoscelis					1	
Hyla versicolor	1		7		46	
Pseudacris crucifer			3		8	
Pseudacris feriarum	1		1		2	
Rana catesbeiana						3
Rana clamitans					30	2
Rana palustris			1			4
Rana sylvatica					2	
Salamanders						
Ambystoma maculatum	1		1		37	
Ambystoma opacum	3				121	
Ambystoma talpoideum					114	
Desmognathus fuscus						4
Eurycea cirrigera			4			8
Eurycea guttolineata						2
Hemidactylium scutatum		1	1			
Notophthalmus viridescens			1		3	
Plethodon cylindraceus			1			
Plethodon cinereus			1			
Turtles						
Chelydra serpentina						1
Chrysemys picta						2
Kinosternon subrubrum					1	
Terrapene carolina		1	11			
Lizards						
Eumeces fasciatus	3	1	4		1	
Sceloporus undulatus	3	1	3	1		
Snakes						
Carphophis amoenus	1	3	5	1		
Coluber constrictor	1					
Diadophis punctatus			10			
Elaphe obsoleta	3					
Nerodia sipedon						2
Regina septemvittata						2
Storeria dekayi			1			
Thamnophis sirtalis		1				
Total	19	8	56	3	366	30

[1] Habitat types include: Grasslands (GRA), Mixed hardwoods and pine (MHP), Mixed hardwoods (MHW), Mixed pine (MPI), Impoundments (IMP), Floodplain Pools (FDPL), and Stream (STR),

Discussion

Inventory

Amphibians and reptiles are highly seasonal animals whose activity patterns respond to changes in climate, temperature, and precipitation. Thus, a complete inventory of amphibians and reptiles can be a challenge during short-term surveys. Rainfall in 2002 was below normal for most months (departure from normal averaged -0.137. cm [-0.054 in], Appomattox weather station, NOAA Climate Data Center, Asheville, NC). These somewhat dry conditions likely influenced the encounter probability and capture success of amphibian and reptile species at APCO during the primary phase of this inventory. Rainfall in 2003 was generally normal to above normal, except in January when precipitation total was nearly 5 cm (2 in) below normal; average departure from normal February–December was 7.9 cm (3.1 in); January departure was -5.79 cm (-2.28 in). In 2004, precipitation was below normal for January–May (average departure was -3.12 cm [-1.23 in]), but above normal for the rest of the year (average departure was 2.54 cm (1.00 in). These variable precipitation patterns had some effect on encounter rates of some amphibians and many of the reptiles. Most snakes, in particular, are very secretive and active only when surface conditions are especially suited. Thus, some of the species likely to be present in APCO were missed in this inventory due to our not being present when the weather conditions were suitable for these difficult-to-find species.

Notwithstanding the climatic limitations, the species encountered during this survey represent a robust list for all groups of amphibians and reptiles, except snakes. Most of the frog species were found during both years of inventories. The success for salamanders (83.3% according to results and tables) is a result of finding ephemeral pools and freshwater springs and seeps at APCO in which several species usually occur. We found two fully terrestrial species, red-backed salamander (*Plethodon cinereus*) and white-spotted slimy salamander (*P. cylindraceus*), but only one of each. This suggests that the hardwood forests have not reached maturity enough to provide the leaf litter and soil depth to allow large populations to build up. This situation, in turn, is a function of the heavy use history of the landscape in this area. The percentage for lizards was only 40% with two of the five expected species encountered at APCO. One species (*Eumeces laticeps*) may not occur in the park due to historical land use (they require mature trees). The other species not encountered, *Scincella lateralis* (Table 1), may be due to the extreme dry conditions or distribution patchiness. The four turtle species we encountered are commonly found in forested landscapes and slow-moving streams and rivers in this region.

Only eight of the 17 species of snakes expected to occur at APCO were documented during the 2003–2004 inventory. Snake species that were not encountered, but were expected to occur at APCO include the northern copperhead, corn snake (*Elaphe guttata*), eastern hog-nosed snake (*Heterodon platirhinos*), mole kingsnake (*Lampropeltis calligaster*), eastern kingsnake (*Lampropeltis getula*), rough greensnake (*Opheodrys* aestivus), red-bellied snake (*Storeria occipitomaculata*), eastern ribbonsnake (*Thamnophis sauritus*), and smooth earthsnake (*Virginia valeriae*). Additional field trips and chance observations in favorable weather conditions would be required to add more snake species to the park's list. Many snakes are active for only short periods of time during favorable weather, usually warm and wet periods (Wright and Wright 1957; Gibbons and Semlitsch 1987). Few species of snakes move with sufficient frequency to be encountered when it is dry. Snakes in general can be especially hard to survey; many are secretive and occur in limited numbers (Gibbons et al. 1997). Leiden et al. (1999) demonstrated with multiple techniques that 66% of the total snake species expected were caught in the first 75 days of sampling, but that an additional 325 days of sampling would be required to collect 90% of the total number expected. Whiteman et al. (1995) and Gibbons et al. (1997) showed that it took over 22 years to discover one snake species on the Savannah River site, an area that has been intensively studied for over 40 years.

Based on distribution patterns of amphibian and reptile species in Maryland (Mitchell 1994; Conant and Collins 1998; Mitchell and Reay 1999), all but one of the species encountered during this survey were expected to occur in APCO. The unexpected species was the Cope's gray treefrog, a species identical in appearance to the eastern gray treefrog, discernible by vocalization only. It occurs in the eastern Piedmont and Coastal Plain in Virginia, as well as along the Virginia/North Carolina state line and in far southwestern Virginia (Mitchell and Reay 1999). Only one was heard calling on one night. Additional survey work needs to be done to determine if there is a reproducing population of this treefrog in APCO. The audio call represents a new county record for this species (Mitchell and Reay 1999); however, a specimen or photograph would have to be obtained before it can be accepted by the scientific community.

The mole salamander is listed by the Virginia Department of Game and Inland Fisheries as a species of special concern. The discovery of this species in APCO is significant and represents a new county record. I discovered two populations, one in the riparian zone along the Appomattox River north of U.S. Rt. 24 and another in the Tibbs Ice pond. Both areas provide the essential ephemeral pool habitat used by this and the other two ambystomatids for breeding. Adults of these salamanders spend only a short time in these breeding pools. Otherwise, they live the rest of their lives in the surrounding landscape, most importantly in the hardwood forest floor. Adults and metamorphs travel long distances from the breeding pool to forest refugia, over 200 m (656 ft) (Pauley et al. 2000). An average of 165 m (541 ft) was calculated for this group of salamanders from several literature sources by Semlitsch and Jensen (2001). The larvae remain in the pools for 2–3 months, then metamorphose into juveniles. Like adults, they move considerable distances into the forest and remain there until maturity when they return to breeding pools.

Sampling Method Efficiency

Because amphibians and reptiles are notoriously secretive animals, successful species documentation depends upon the use of multiple capture techniques in both wetland and terrestrial habitats (Corn and Bury 1990; Heyer et al. 1994; Ryan et al. 2002). Determining which method(s) are most effective depends on the goal of the inventory, as well as the behaviors and habitats of target species expected to be encountered. Visual encounter surveys often detect the greatest numbers of species, as was the case in this survey, detecting 30 of the 33 species encountered (Table 2). It is important to keep in mind though, when choosing to use VES, that this survey method will not provide quantitative data useful for estimating population size or structure, primary habitat preferences, or habitat use during different life stages or distribution. It is also important to note that visual encounter surveys are difficult to replicate in future efforts, as they lack rigor from a sampling and statistical perspective, and are essentially qualitative rather than quantitative. Their primary usefulness is in assessing species richness of the study area.

The results of this survey also indicate that methods vary in their effectiveness at detecting different species, even those within the same taxonomic group such as frogs. Considering the diversity of amphibian and reptiles and the variability in their size, modes of reproduction, patterns of habitat use, degree of habitat specialization, and life history, this is expected. To account for this, a generalized, multi-habitat inventory should always incorporate a number of different methods. Choice of methods will depend to a certain extent on the relative importance placed on detecting species presence versus generating quantitative estimates of abundance, population size and structure, and habitat comparisons, as well as what the potential species are. Based on the APCO inventory, audio surveys, dipnet surveys, and minnow traps, when augmented by visual encounter surveys, were most effective for the generalized inventory of this park.

For frogs, the combination of audio, dipnet, and VES surveys proved to be the most effective documentation method. Use of minnow traps is an effective way to inventory salamander larvae and frog tadpoles and they should always be considered when developing inventory plans. Other survey methods, such as road surveys, can be an effective technique for documenting snakes, turtles and frogs, although success depends greatly on weather and seasonal activity patterns. The road survey method proved unreliable in APCO.

One method that should be considered specifically for the documentation of snakes is coverboard surveys. The use of coverboards, quarter sheets of plywood, roofing tin, or other similar material laid out in selected areas on the ground, could have been used to potentially enhance snake capture success at APCO. Coverboards were not used in this study as it was assumed that there would be sufficient logs and other surface cover objects available throughout the park for searching. Unfortunately there were fewer natural cover objects available than expected in areas that might have harbored small snakes. Other methods that could potentially be used to survey snakes include glueboards, but these can result in the death of animals so are not highly recommended, or drift fences with pitfall traps. Drift fence and pitfall traps require a large effort to install and operate (Gibbons and Semlitsch 1981). In the future, additional work to document the snake fauna at APCO should include the use of coverboards placed in selected habitats around the park.

Species/Habitat Associations

Protection of selected habitats could allow viable populations of native amphibians and reptiles to persist in APCO. Amphibians and reptiles function in a landscape context (Semlitsch 2003), and a mix of habitat types is essential for their existence in the park. Long-term preservation of the amphibian and reptile populations at APCO will require the management and maintenance of a variety of habitat types. Factors that may impact this mosaic should be identified and addressed in the park management plan. Habitats that support relatively unique assemblages of these vertebrates include hardwood forests, Tibbs Ice Pond, the riparian area and floodplain pools, and the Appomattox River.

The habitat classification used in the current study was based on general field descriptions and is indicative of the ecological conditions favorable to amphibians and reptiles (e.g., Wright and Wright 1957; Martof et al. 1980; Mitchell 1994; Conant and Collins 1998). These animals rely more on the environmental structure (shelter, temperature, relative humidity) provided by plant community environments rather than individual plant species composition (pers. obs.). Most amphibians and reptiles use multiple habitat types that are adjacent to one another during their daily and seasonal movements (e.g., Reinert 1993; Buhlmann 2001; Semlitsch 2003), and may travel 1 km (0.6 mi) or more (e.g., Gregory et al. 1987; Semlitsch 1998; Semlitsch and Bodie 1998; Pauley et al. 2000). Some habitats may be used by species only during movements from one primary habitat to another, and other species can move among several habitat types in a single day or season. It is important to remember that a record in a single habitat type may only be a snapshot of habitat preference by a species. Only detailed studies of movements using radio-telemetry can reveal all the habitats used by a species in a given area (e.g., Reinert 1993; Carter et al. 1999).

Important components of the existing APCO landscape necessary for maintaining amphibian and reptile species include the matrix or combination of freshwater seasonal ponds and hardwood forest habitats throughout the park, but especially in the Appomattox River floodplain; this habitat contains several ephemeral pools that are essential breeding habitats for three ambystomatid salamander species (spotted, marbled, mole). These predominately subterranean salamanders spend most of their lives in the forested areas surrounding the ephemeral or seasonal ponds in which they breed. The hardwood forests contain an underground tunnel matrix required by these salamanders that seldom create their own burrows. These species must have a combination of habitat types, such as the ephemeral or seasonal ponds and surrounding hardwood forest, in order to meet their life history requirements. Loss of one of these habitat types could result in the loss of these species from the park. Appropriate corridors connecting hardwood forests and ephemeral or seasonal ponds are essential landscape features that greatly influence the viability of ambystomatid salamander populations in APCO.

The amount of terrestrial habitat used by ambystomatid salamanders depends on the distances these animals travel away from their breeding pool or pond. Averages from several studies has shown that at least 164.3 m (540 ft) of terrestrial habitat is required around a breeding pool to protect 95% of an *Ambystoma* salamander population (Semlitsch 1998). Most amphibians move considerably further. For example, many frogs and salamanders have been documented to travel over a kilometer (3,280 ft [0.6 mi]) from their aquatic breeding sites (Pauley et al. 2000). Thus, effective amphibian conservation will require preserving several hundred meters of appropriate terrestrial habitat (specifically mature hardwood forests) around much of the breeding pools or ponds in the park. In the best of circumstances, preserving areas composed of terrestrial habitat with an imbedded complex of ephemeral or seasonal ponds is ideal.

Another important factor to consider in the conservation of amphibians is their movement between breeding pools and ponds in order to maintain viable populations. Maintaining viable populations of amphibians in the park will require that these animals be able to disperse across habitats and among breeding areas and that dispersal corridors be included in any species management plan. As recently discussed in the literature, habitat conservation strategies for amphibians must include the maintenance and preservation of a core habitat composed of breeding pools or ponds and the terrestrial habitat surrounding them (165 m [540 ft]average) surrounded by an additional buffer zone (Semlitsch and Jensen 2001).

Aquatic habitats (Tibbs Ice Pond, floodplain pools) support a diverse array of species, with many species using more than one of these habitats in APCO. Ambystomatid salamanders, treefrogs, and ranid frogs were the dominant fauna found in the park's primary impoundment and floodplain pools, while several streamside salamanders and freshwater turtles were found primarily in stream habitats.

Although habitat type was collected as part of the inventory conducted at APCO, this information can only provide a simple snapshot of habitat types that amphibian and reptile species use in this park. It is important to remember that it would be incorrect to say that most of the species were captured or documented in Mixed-Hardwood habitat (MHW) as shown in Table 3, without considering the number and extent of the embedded seasonal ponds within those habitats. MHP and MHW habitats without the seasonal ponds would most likely support a completely different assemblage of amphibian and reptile species than what was recorded during this inventory. Again, it must be stressed, that when considering management of areas that support herpetological species within the park, a complete picture of the existing landscape matrix must be included. The habitat information collected as part of this inventory can only provide a general picture of where specific amphibian and reptile species might be found in the park, and no quantitative analysis can be done to rank the use of habitat types by species.

Management Issues

Effective amphibian and reptile management first requires identification of threats. The threats to these vertebrates on APCO include mortality from vehicular traffic, human disturbance or killing, subsidized predators, and habitat loss or alteration. Removal of animals by humans for personal pets or the commercial pet trade constitutes an unknown threat level, as there is no data to evaluate this impact. Habitat loss is not considered a major threat at APCO. Future plans for alteration of areas of park land that may include habitat loss should be reviewed thoroughly and losses should be prevented when possible. Specific areas to which special attention should be paid include the impoundment, the floodplain zone and the Appomattox River, and the full-canopy hardwood forests. These habitats should be maintained as natural areas with amphibians and reptiles in mind. Vehicular traffic on U.S. Rt. 24 remains a threat to amphibians and reptiles crossing this road. An evaluation of the magnitude of these threats should be undertaken and measures put in place to control the mortality of these animals.

Conclusions and Management Recommendations

Habitat Restricted Species

Most of the herpetological species found at APCO are those that occur throughout the Virginia Piedmont. Many of these species use a variety of habitats during daily movements, as well as seasonal movements to breeding pools and ponds. Most species can be considered as habitat generalists except for the stream salamanders and the pool-breeding ambystomatid salamanders. Additional inventory work on each individual habitat type should be considered to better understand the abundance and distributions of amphibians and reptiles within them.

Management of these two populations of mole salamanders requires protection of Tibbs Ice Pond and the pools on the Appomattox River floodplain as well as the surrounding terrestrial habitat. We do not know the maximum distances these salamanders will travel from the pools, but taking the average from Semlitsch and Jensen (2001) should be a reasonable guide. Maintenance of the hydrologies of these pools is also critical. A primary reason ambystomatid salamanders use these pools for breeding is the lack of fish. The seasonal (summer) drying of the pools ensures that fish do not survive should they be introduced naturally or by humans. Thus, management should include not only protection and management of the aquatic and terrestrial habitats, but also control of human impacts to these habitats. Further study is needed to determine the distances traveled by these salamanders, their life history parameters (especially annual survivorship), and whether the two populations are connected by exchange of individuals. The latter is unlikely, given the distance between the two, but the question needs to be ruled out. This can be done through a long-term mark-recapture study or by analysis of genetic markers. Finally, the locations of these populations should not be made available to collectors or anyone without special need to know.

The problem of the mortality of reptiles and amphibians, especially turtles and some snakes, on U.S. Rt. 24 needs to be evaluated. A study of mortality rates, primary crossing points, and the species involved is recommended so that places that could benefit from proper fencing or perhaps construction of culverts with fencing (small ecopassages) can be identified. Individuals of some of the amphibian and reptile populations may need to cross over the road to reach important habitats, such as overwintering sites or breeding sites. Solutions to such roadkill problems are not easily resolved due to the dynamics of animal behavior and potential costs. However, the magnitude of the problem should be evaluated to determine if remediation is really needed.

Amphibians and Reptiles as Indicators of Ecosystem Health

During a recent study on box turtles it was found that nearly all turtles captured in parts of Virginia had high levels of organochlorine pesticide in their systems. Because box turtles are so long-lived they can accumulate chemicals from the environment. A good example is the development of aural (ear) abscesses as a result of vitamin A deficiency caused by organochlorine pesticide contamination (Holladay et al. 2001; Brown et al. 2004). Because of these recent studies on box turtles it is becoming more and more apparent that they may be excellent indicators of ecosystem condition and health. During this inventory at APCO, no turtles with aural abscesses were found, suggesting that this may not currently be a problem at APCO. Environmental contamination by pollutants from increased human development of the area around APCO may produce such problems, and could be additionally monitored by annual surveys of box turtle population conditions at the park.

Ecotoxicology studies of herbicide and pesticide effects on amphibians have not been thorough and often use only a laboratory species not found in North America (McDiarmid and Mitchell 2000). Spraying herbicides and pesticides in and over terrestrial and wetland habitats could produce harmful results to amphibian populations, especially at the larval stage. The use of larvacides for mosquito control (West Nile virus) in wetlands such as seasonal ponds is also likely to be harmful to larval-staged amphibians. Decisions to use chemicals for natural resource management should thus be made with extreme caution, and larval populations monitored both prior to and post spraying of pesticides. Nearly all commercial pesticides and herbicides are now considered harmful to amphibian larvae and adults (Relyea and Mills 2001; Relyea 2004, 2005). Broadcast applications of commercial chemicals in APCO should be evaluated fully with all impacts in mind before being allowed to be used.

Education

Educational materials should be developed on the ecology, flora and fauna, and their interactions with human history at APCO. Such materials will properly advise visitors of the value of this park to natural resources and instruct them on the context within which the historical actions took place.

Additional Inventory Work

Additional species documentation work would be of value for all species of amphibians and reptiles in APCO. Such documentation provided by park staff and visitor observations could add several species to the known list. Further work to document snake species at APCO should include the use of coverboards as part of its sampling plan. Additional documentation to add to the overall amphibian and reptile species list for APCO could be accomplished in three ways: (1) routine accumulation of digital photographs of road-kills, especially snakes, with appropriate documentation (date and location); (2) use of several coverboard arrays monitored periodically; and (3) use of natural history (animal) sighting cards filled out by knowledgeable visitors. Initiation of the latter program would result in a valuable source of information for natural resource management staff if accompanied by verifiable information such as a photograph or specimen. In addition, further herpetological work at APCO could include methods for acquiring species abundance and detailed distribution information for all species documented during this inventory.

The copperhead, the only venomous snake in the area, is not a common snake at APCO and was not found during our survey. Their low occurrence frequency and apparent spotty distribution in the area suggests that education may be the only reasonable approach that could be used by park personnel to address their presence and this potential threat to humans. Park personnel should be trained on field emergency treatment of copperhead snakebite, realizing that such bites are not fatal.

Habitat Management

Long-term habitat management at APCO would benefit if management issues and potential construction impacts were viewed within the context of the park's landscape matrix as a whole. Any change to mixed hardwood forests, the ephemeral pond, and river floodplain at APCO, for example, may have consequences to three ambystomatid salamander species, the streamside salamander complex, and the box turtle populations. Many individuals of the latter species are long-lived (30–100 years old, Dodd 2001).

Mowing is a weekly, if not daily, activity at APCO. Such operations are well known for killing box turtles. Thus, blade height on mowers should be set at least 6 inches high or higher to avoid killing box turtles that may be walking across lawns.

Specific habitats should be monitored at APCO for the occurrence and persistence of amphibians and reptiles, including the ephemeral pond, floodplain pools, and mature hardwoods. Hardwood forest habitats are critical areas for some amphibians and reptiles. Forests with full to partial canopy and a well-defined forest floor with downed woody debris and leaves provide important microhabitat for several species and should be maintained with the concept of "old growth" in mind.

Tibbs Ice Pond should be maintained as a small breeding pond for amphibians, especially the three ambystomatid salamanders. Fish should not be stocked in this pond. If any fish are present they should be removed; this may take an effort to draw down the pond or wait for a serious drought to help the process. Adjacent emergent vegetation and cattails should be encouraged and maintained as refugia for frogs. Do not clear the hardwood forest adjacent to this pond. It may be advisable to clear some of the briar and shrub undergrowth from portions of the pond, especially where it is too thick for reptiles to pass through.

The Appomattox River and its riparian floodplain should be maintained in as natural a state as possible. Land clearing and other activities should be evaluated as to their effects on these sensitive habitats before such activities take place. Such activities should be avoided if at all possible.

A comprehensive natural habitat management plan for the conservation of native species and their habitats should be developed for APCO. Its natural history has received little to no attention. A management plan for this historic site would ensure that this area is maintained in sufficient natural conditions to allow the persistence of the native amphibian and reptile fauna. The working/research committee for such a plan could include experts in all floral and faunal groups, as well as forest and wetland conservation biologists.

Vehicles and Recreational Activities

Garber and Burger (1995) found that opening an area to recreation resulted in the complete loss of a wood turtle (*Clemmys insculpta*) population, caused primarily by removal of turtles by humans and dogs. Humans pick up box, wood, and other turtles and will remove them or at least carry them to other locations in the park. Removal of even one mature adult female results in the loss of a critically important reproductive individual to the population. Populations of such long-lived species depend entirely on their mature adults to remain stable or increase. Their removal will result in population decline and extirpation. Areas of the park where there tend to be high concentrations of box turtles, such river floodplains and mature hardwood forests, should be evaluated before opening them to recreational activities.

Rates of mortality on park roads are unknown, but could be significant for some species. Knowing these rates and better understanding the seasonality of road mortalities in the park will help resource managers to better manage potential problem areas and allow steps to be taken to minimize vehicular mortality on park roads. Unfortunately, a major highway bisects the park and little can be done to prevent road mortality there. If there are areas where animal mortality is commonplace, then evaluation of the potential for an ecopassages may be warranted.

Exotics and Subsidized Predators

Scavenging/predatory mammals usually exist at higher population densities in areas of high human use due to garbage and discarded food and structures as shelters. Raccoons, notorious for killing and eating turtle adults and eggs in nests, can dramatically decrease populations of these species. They also eat frogs and any other amphibian or reptile they can catch. Animals that qualify as subsidized predators include raccoons, foxes (*Urocyon cinereoargenteus*), opossums (*Didelphis virginiana*), skunks (*Mephitis mephitis*), and crows (*Corvus brachyrhynchos*) (Mitchell and Klemens 2000). The introduced house cat (free-ranging and feral [*Felis silvestris*]) is also included in this category because they kill large numbers of native animals (Mitchell and Beck 1992). Populations of raccoons and other subsidized predators, especially cats, are likely contributing to declines in some native species populations at APCO. An evaluation of the size of the feral cat and raccoon populations in the park, as well as mapping their distribution in relation to park use activities, should be undertaken. Identification of primary turtle nesting sites and evaluation of nest loss to raccoons and other subsidized predators should also be conducted. Such information would allow informed management decisions about control of the cat and raccoon populations.

Captive-raised or captive-bred amphibians and reptiles should not be released at APCO under any circumstances. It is against Virginia Department of Game and Inland Fisheries law for any species to be released after being held in captivity. The potential for disease introduction is growing and every effort should be made to avoid contamination from exotics or native species from other areas. Captivity often induces stress and influences development of disease. The public should not be allowed to release any animals that have been in captivity, and park management should educate park visitors on this issue.

Literature Cited

Blomberg, S., and R. Shine. 1996. Reptiles. Pages 218–226 *in* W. J. Sutherland, editor. Ecological Census Techniques, a Handbook. Cambridge University Press. Cambridge, UK.

Braswell, A. L. 1988. Preliminary report on a survey of the herpetofauna of Cape Hatteras National Seashore. Unpublished report submitted to the National Park Service. NC State Museum of Natural Sciences. Raleigh, NC. 13 pp.

Brown, J. D., J. M. Richards, J. Robertson, S. Holladay, and J. M. Sleeman. 2004. Pathology of aural abscesses in free-living box turtles (*Terrapene carolina carolina*). Journal of Wildlife Diseases 40:704–712.

Buhlmann, K. A. 2001. Terrestrial habitat use by aquatic turtles from a seasonally fluctuating wetland: implications for wetland conservation boundaries. Chelonian Conservation and Biology 4:115-127.

Carter, S. L., C. A. Haas, and J. C. Mitchell. 1999. Home range and habitat selection of bog turtles in southwestern Virginia. Journal of Wildlife Management 63:853–860.

Conant, R., and J. T. Collins. 1998. A Field Guide to Reptiles and Amphibians Eastern and Central North America. 3rd expanded edition. Peterson Field Guide Series. Houghton Mifflin Co. Boston, MA. 616 pp.

Corn, P. S., and R. B. Bury. 1990. Sampling methods for terrestrial amphibians and reptiles. U.S.D.A., Forest Service. General Technical Report PNW-GTR-256.

Crother, B. I. (committee chair). 2000. Scientific and standard English names of amphibians and reptiles of North America north of Mexico, with comments regarding confidence in our understanding. SSAR Herpetological Circular 29:1–82.

Dodd, C. K., Jr. 2001. North American Box Turtles, A Natural History. University of Oklahoma Press. Norman, OK. 231 pp.

Forester, D. C. 2000. Amphibian inventory Chesapeake and Ohio Canal and National Historic Park. Unpublished report to the National Park Service. Washington, DC. 62 pp.

Garber, S. D., and J. Burger. 1995. A 20-year study documenting the relationship between turtle decline and human recreation. Ecological Applications 5:1151–1162.

Gibbons, J. W., and R. D. Semlitsch. 1981. Terrestrial drift fences with pitfall traps: an effective technique for quantitative sampling of animal populations. Brimleyana 7:1–16.

Gibbons, J. W., and R. D. Semlitsch. 1987. Activity patterns. Pp. 396–421 *in* R. A. Seigel, J. T. Collins, and S. S. Novak, editors. Snakes: Ecology and Evolutionary Biology. Macmillan Publishing Co. New York, NY.

Gibbons, J. W., V. J. Burke, J. E. Lovich, R. D. Semlitsch, T. D. Tuberville, J. R. Bodie, J. R. Greene, P. H. Niewiarowski, H. H. Whiteman, D. E. Scott, and others. 1997. Perceptions of species abundance, distribution, and diversity: lessons from four decades of sampling on a government-managed reserve. Environmental Management 21:259–268.

Gregory, P. T., J. M. Macartney, and K. W. Larsen. 1987. Spatial patterns and movements. Pages 366–395 *in* R. A. Seigel, J. T. Collins, and S. S. Novak, editors. Snakes: Ecology and Evolutionary Biology. Macmillan Publishing Co. New York, NY.

Heyer, W. R., M. A. Donnelly, R. W. McDiarmid, L. C. Hayek, and M. S. Foster. 1994. Measuring and Monitoring Biological Diversity, Standard Methods for Amphibians. Smithsonian Institution Press. Washington, DC. 364 pp.

Hobson, C. S. 1997. A natural heritage inventory of groundwater invertebrates within the Virginia portions of the George Washington Memorial Parkway including Great Falls Park. Natural Heritage Technical Report 97-9. Virginia Department of Conservation and Recreation, Division of Natural Heritage, Richmond. Unpublished report submitted to the National Park Service. 36 pp. + appendix.

Hobson, C. S. 1998. A natural heritage inventory of the Cheatham and Wormley Pond drainages, Colonial National Historical Park. Natural Heritage Technical Report 98-11. Virginia Department of Conservation and Recreation, Division of Natural Heritage. Richmond, VA. 42 pp. + appendixes.

Holladay, S. D., J. C. Wolf, S. A. Smith, D. E. Jones, and J. L. Robertson. 2001. Aural abscesses in wild-caught box turtles (*Terrapene carolina*): possible role of organochlorine-induced hypervitaminosis A. Ecotoxicology and Environmental Safety 48:99–106.

Jones, K. B. 1986. Amphibians and reptiles. Pages 267–290 *in* A. Y. Cooperrider, R. J. Boyd, and H. R. Stuart, editors. Inventory and Monitoring of Wildlife Habitat. U.S. Dept. of Interior, Bureau of Land Management Service Center. Denver, CO.

Leiden, Y. A., M. E. Dorcas, and J. W. Gibbons. 1999. Herpetofaunal diversity in Coastal Plain communities of South Carolina. Journal of the Elisha Mitchell Scientific Society 115:270–280.

Martof, B. S., W. M. Palmer, J. R. Bailey, and J. R. Harrison, III. 1980. Amphibians and Reptiles of the Carolinas and Virginia. University of North Carolina Press. Chapel Hill, NC. 264 pp.

McDiarmid, R. W., and J. C. Mitchell. 2000. Diversity and distribution of amphibians and reptiles. Pages 15–69 *in* D. W. Sparling, G. Linder, and C. A. Bishop (eds.). Ecotoxicology of Amphibians and Reptiles. Society of Environmental Toxicology and Chemistry. SETAC Press. Pensacola, FL.

Mitchell, J. C. 1994. The Reptiles of Virginia. Smithsonian Institution Press. Washington, DC. 352 pp.

Mitchell, J. C. 2000a. Amphibian Monitoring Methods & Field Guide. Smithsonian National Zoological Park, Conservation Research Center. Front Royal, VA. 56 pp.

Mitchell, J. C. 2000b. Amphibians and reptiles of the National Capital Parks: Review of existing information and inventory methods. Unpublished report to the National Park Service. Washington, DC. 50 pp.

Mitchell, J. C., and J. M. Anderson. 1994. Amphibians and Reptiles of Assateague and Chincoteague Islands. Virginia Museum of Natural History. Martinsville, VA. 120 pp.

Mitchell, J. C., and R. A. Beck. 1992. Free-ranging domestic cat predation on native vertebrates in rural and urban Virginia. Virginia Journal of Science 43:197–207.

Mitchell, J. C., and M. W. Klemens. 2000. Primary and secondary effects of habitat alteration. Pages 5–32 in M. W. Klemens, editor. Turtle Conservation. Smithsonian Institution Press. Washington, DC.

Mitchell, J. C., and K. K. Reay. 1999. Atlas of Amphibians and Reptiles in Virginia. Special Publication Number 1. Virginia Department of Game and Inland Fisheries. Richmond, VA. 122 pp.

Pauley, T. K., J. C. Mitchell, R. R. Buech, and J. J. Moriarty. 2000. Ecology and management of riparian habitats for amphibians and reptiles. Pp. 169–192 in E. S. Verry, J. W. Hornbeck, and C. A. Dolloff (eds.). Riparian Management in Forests of the Continental Eastern United States. Lewis Publishers. Boca Raton, FL.

Radford, A. E., H. E. Ahles, and C. R. Bell. 1968. Manual of the Vascular Flora of the Carolinas. University of North Carolina Press. Chapel Hill, NC. 1,183 pp.

Reinert, H. K. 1993. Habitat selection in snakes. Pages 201-240 in R. A. Seigel and J. T. Collins (eds.). Snakes: Ecology and Behavior. McGraw Hill, Inc. New York, NY.

Relyea, R. A. 2004. Growth and survival of five amphibian species exposed to combinations of pesticides. Environmental Toxicology and Chemistry 23:1737–1742.

Relyea, R. A., and N. Mills. 2001. Predator-induced stress makes the pesticide carbaryl more deadly to gray treefrog tadpoles (*Hyla versicolor*). Proceeding of the National Academy of Science 98:2491–2496.

Relyea, R. A. 2005. The lethal impact of Roundup on aquatic and terrestrial amphibians. Ecological Applications 15:1118–1124.

Ryan, T. J., T. Philippi, Y. A. Leiden, M. E. Dorcas, T. B. Wigley, and J. W. Gibbons. 2002. Monitoring herpetofauna in a managed forest landscape: effects of habitat types and census techniques. Forest Ecology and Management 167:83–90.

Semlitsch, R. D. 1998. Biological delineation of terrestrial buffer zones for pond-breeding salamanders. Conservation Biology 12:1113–1119.

Semlitsch, R. D. 2003. Conservation of pond-breeding amphibians. Pages. 8–23 *in* R.D. Semlitsch, editor. Amphibian Conservation. Smithsonian Institution Press. Washington, DC.

Semlitsch, R. D., and J. R. Bodie. 1998. Are small, isolated wetlands expendable? Conservation Biology 12:1129–1133.

Semlitsch, R. D., and J. B. Jensen. 2001. Core habitat, not buffer zone. National Wetlands Newsletter 23(4):5–6, 11.

Tuberville, T. D., J. D. Williams, M. E. Dorcas, and J. W. Gibbons. 2005. Herpetofaunal species richness of southeastern national parks. Southeastern Naturalist 4(3):537–569.

Whiteman, H. H., T. M. Mills, D. E. Scott, and J. W. Gibbons. 1995. Confirmation of a range extension for the pine woods snake (*Rhadinaea flavilata*). Herpetological Review 26:158.

Wright, A. H., and A. A. Wright. 1957. Handbook of Snakes of the United States and Canada. 2 Vols. Cornell University Press. Ithaca, NY. 1105 pp.

Appendix A. Potential checklist of the amphibians and reptiles of Appomattox Court House National Historical Park. This checklist is based on known distributions of amphibians and reptiles in Virginia. The species actually occurring in APCO are a subset of this list.

CLASS AMPHIBIA	
Order Anura	**Frogs and Toads**
Family Bufonidae	Toads
Bufo americanus americanus Holbrook	eastern American toad
Bufo fowleri Hinckley	Fowler's toad
Family Hylidae	Treefrogs
Acris crepitans crepitans Baird	eastern cricket frog
Hyla chrysoscelis Cope	Cope's gray treefrog
Hyla versicolor LeConte	eastern gray treefrog
Pseudacris crucifer crucifer Wied-Neuwied	northern spring peeper
Pseudacris feriarum feriarum (Baird)	upland chorus frog
Family Microhylidae	Microhylids
Gastrophryne carolinensis (Holbrook)	eastern narrow-mouthed toad
Family Pelobatidae	Spadefoot Toads
Scaphiopus holbrookii (Harlan)	Eastern Spadefoot
Family Ranidae	True Frogs
Rana catesbeiana Shaw	American bullfrog
Rana clamitans melanota (Rafinesque)	northern green frog
Rana palustris LeConte	pickerel frog
Rana sylvatica LeConte	wood frog
Order Caudata	**Salamanders**
Family Ambystomatidae	Mole Salamanders
Ambystoma maculatum (Shaw)	spotted salamander
Ambystoma opacum (Gravenhorst)	marbled salamander
Ambystoma talpoideum (Holbrook)	mole salamander
Family Plethodontidae	Lungless Salamanders
Desmognathus fuscus (Rafinesque)	northern dusky salamander
Eurycea cirrigera (Green)	southern two-lined salamander
Hemidactylium scutatum (Schlegel)	four-toed salamander
Plethodon cinereus (Green)	red-backed salamander
Plethodon cylindraceus (Harlan)	white-spotted slimy sal.
Pseudotriton montanus montanus Baird	eastern mud salamander
Pseudotriton ruber ruber (Latreille)	northern red salamander
Family Salamandridae	True Salamanders
Notophthalmus viridescens viridescens (Rafinesque)	red-spotted newt
CLASS REPTILIA	
Order Testudines	**Turtles**
Family Chelydridae	snapping turtles
Chelydra serpentina serpentina (Linnaeus)	eastern snapping turtle
Family Emydidae	Pond Turtles
Chrysemys picta picta (Schneider)	eastern painted turtle
Terrapene carolina carolina (Linnaeus)	eastern box turtle
Family Kinosternidae	Mud and Musk Turtles
Kinosternon subrubrum subrubrum (Lacepède)	eastern mud turtle
Sternotherus odoratus (Latreille)	eastern musk turtle

Order Squamata	**Lizards, Snakes and Amphisbaenians**
Suborder Sauria	**Lizards**
Family Phrynosomatidae	Sceloporine Lizards
Sceloporus undulatus hyacinthinus (Green)	northern fence lizard
Family Scincidae	Skinks
Eumeces fasciatus (Linnaeus)	five-lined skink
Eumeces laticeps (Schneider)	broad-headed skink
Scincella lateralis (Say)	little brown skink
Family Teiidae	Tegus and Whiptails
Cnemidophorus sexlineatus sexlineatus (Linnaeus)	eastern six-lined racerunner
Suborder Serpentes	**Snakes**
Family Colubridae	Colubrids
Carphophis amoenus amoenus (Say)	eastern wormsnake
Coluber constrictor constrictor Linnaeus	northern black racer
Diadophis punctatus edwardsii (Merrem)	northern ring-necked snake
Elaphe guttata (Linnaeus)	corn snake
Elaphe obsoleta obsoleta (Say)	black ratsnake
Heterodon platirhinos Latreille	eastern hog-nosed snake
Lampropeltis calligaster rhombomaculata (Holbrook)	mole kingsnake
Lampropeltis getula getula (Linnaeus)	eastern kingsnake
Nerodia sipedon sipedon (Linnaeus)	northern watersnake
Opheodrys aestivus (Linnaeus)	rough greensnake
Regina septemvittata (Say)	queen snake
Storeria dekayi dekayi (Holbrook)	northern brownsnake
Storeria occipitomaculata occipitomaculata (Storer)	northern red-bellied snake
Thamnophis sauritus sauritus (Linnaeus)	eastern ribbonsnake
Thamnophis sirtalis sirtalis (Linnaeus)	common gartersnake
Virginia valeriae valeriae Baird and Girard	eastern smooth earthsnake
Family Viperidae	Vipers and Pitvipers
Agkistrodon contortrix mokasen (Palisot de Beauvois)	northern copperhead

* Observed by Joe Mitchell and field crew 2003–2004

Appendix B. Amphibian and reptile survey dates and sampling method at Appomattox Court House National Historical Park, 2003 and 2004.

Method	Dates of field trips
VES	2002: May 9
	2003: Apr. 30, Jun. 2, 3, Jul. 9, 10, Aug. 13, Sep. 7
	2004: May 23, Jul. 31
Dipnets	2003: Mar. 13, Apr. 30, Jun. 2, Jul. 9, Sep. 7
Minnow traps	2003: Jun. 2-3, Jul. 9-10, 10-11
Turtle traps	2003: Jun. 2-3
Road Survey	2003: Apr. 30
Audio	2002: May 9
	2003: Mar. 13, 21, Apr. 30

Appendix C. List of photographic images of amphibians and reptiles for Appomattox Court House National Historical Park. All images (jpg files) are coded by APCO-Number and Scientific name (e.g., APCO-1 B. *americanus*). All images from APCO unless otherwise specified.

Image #	Scientific name	Common name	Notes
	Frogs		
APCO-1	*Bufo americanus*	American toad	
APCO-2	*Hyla chrysoscelis*	Cope's gray treefrog	
APCO-3	*Hyla versicolor*	eastern gray treefrog	
APCO-4	*Pseudacris crucifer*	northern spring peeper	
APCO-5	*Pseudacris feriarum*	upland chorus frog	
APCO-6	*Rana catesbeiana*	American bullfrog	
APCO-7	*Rana clamitans*	northern green frog	Tadpoles only in APCO, image from Ft. Lee
APCO-8	*Rana palustris*	pickerel frog	
APCO-9	*Rana sylvatica*	wood frog	
	Salamanders		
APCO-10	*Ambystoma maculatum*	spotted salamander	
APCO-11	*Ambystoma opacum*	marbled salamander	Juvenile
APCO-12	*Ambystoma talpoideum*	mole salamander	
APCO-13	*Desmognathus fuscus*	northern dusky salamander	
APCO-14	*Eurycea cirrigera*	southern two-lined salamander	
APCO-15	*Eurycea guttolineata*	three-lined salamander	
APCO-16	*Hemidactylium scutatum*	four-toed salamander	
APCO-17	*Notophthalmus viridescens*	red-spotted newt	
APCO-18	*Plethodon cinereus*	red-backed salamander	
APCO-19	*Plethodon cylindraceus*	white-spotted slimy salamander	
	Turtles		
APCO-20	*Chelydra serpentina*	snapping turtle	
APCO-21	*Chrysemys picta*	eastern painted turtle	
APCO-22	*Kinosternon subrubrum*	eastern mud turtle	
APCO-23	*Terrapene carolina*	eastern box turtle	2 images
	Lizards		
APCO-24	*Eumeces fasciatus*	five-lined skink	Obs only at APCO, Image from COLO
APCO-25	*Sceloporus undulatus*	northern fence lizard	
	Snakes		
APCO-26	*Carphophis amoenus*	eastern worm snake	
APCO-27	*Coluber constrictor*	northern black racer	Obs only at APCO, Juv, Image from Ft. Lee
APCO-28	*Diadophis punctatus*	northern ring-necked snake	
APCO-29	*Elaphe obsoleta*	black ratsnake	
APCO-30	*Nerodia sipedon*	northern watersnake	
APCO-31	*Regina septemvittata*	queen snake	
APCO-32	*Storeria dekayi*	northern brownsnake	
APCO-33	*Thamnophis sirtalis*	eastern gartersnake	

As the nation's primary conservation agency, the Department of the Interior has responsibility for most of our nationally owned public land and natural resources. This includes fostering sound use of our land and water resources; protecting our fish, wildlife, and biological diversity; preserving the environmental and cultural values of our national parks and historical places; and providing for the enjoyment of life through outdoor recreation. The department assesses our energy and mineral resources and works to ensure that their development is in the best interests of all our people by encouraging stewardship and citizen participation in their care. The department also has a major responsibility for American Indian reservation communities and for people who live in island territories under U.S. administration.

NPS D-082 September 2006